Diving at the Pool

Story by Kaye Baillie
Illustrations by Claire Bridge

The school swim meet
was going to be held
in three weeks.
Yasmin's class arrived at the pool
to practice.

"I'm going to try out
for every race," said Sarah,
as they went to get changed.
"Which ones do you want to be in?"

"I don't really want to be
in any of the races," answered Yasmin.

"I thought you liked freestyle,"
said Sarah.
"You are good at swimming now."

"But I can't dive," said Yasmin.
"How can I be in a freestyle race
if I can't dive?"

Yasmin stood at the end of the pool
and looked down at the water.
I'll try once more,
she thought.
She put her arms out in front of her,
and flopped into the pool
with a splash.

"That was a funny dive!"
said one of the boys, and he grinned.
He pretended to dive like Yasmin.

Yasmin felt very embarrassed.
Her face was red.

That evening,
Yasmin could hardly eat her dinner.

"What's the matter?" her father asked.

"I'm quite good at swimming,"
said Yasmin, "but I'm afraid to dive.
Every time I try,
I think I'm going to hurt myself.
I look silly in front of the others."

Dad said,
"I know someone
who is good at diving.
She could teach you."
He looked at Mom.

Mom smiled at Yasmin.
"I'll give you a few lessons
this weekend," she said.

On Saturday, Yasmin and Mom
arrived at the pool early.
They had it all to themselves.

"Watch how I hold my arms
and balance on the side of the pool,"
said Mom.
She made a smooth dive
into the water.

"That was great, Mom," said Yasmin,
"but I don't want to try just yet."

Mom nodded.
"Just watch how I do it," she said.

Yasmin watched carefully,
but she was still feeling scared.

"You make it look so easy,"
said Yasmin.

"Come on," said Mom.
"Why don't you try?
Remember, the water is deep,
so you can't hurt yourself."

Mom showed Yasmin
how to point her arms.
Yasmin bent her knees and jumped.
She flopped into the water
with a splash.

"Mom, I **still** can't do it,"
cried Yasmin.
She was very disappointed.

"This time,
pretend that you have springs
on your feet," said Mom,
"and that you can see
a treasure chest
at the bottom of the pool."

Yasmin got ready.
She stood still for a moment,
then she leaped into the air
and dived into the pool.

Yasmin moved smoothly
through the water.
"I did it!" she cried,
when she came to the surface.
"I can dive!"

"Yes," said Mom.
"That was a lovely dive."

Yasmin and her mother went back
to the pool during the week.
Yasmin practiced her diving
again and again.

One morning,
Dad came with them.
"I'm really proud of you, Yasmin,"
he said. "You can dive very well."

Then it was the week of the meet.
The children had three more days
to practice their swimming.

Yasmin stood at the end of the pool
and dived into the water.

"That was great!" called Sarah.
"Now we can be
in the freestyle race together."